MAN SPY

Photo Anthology by Peter Slater

I remember this guy who worked for my Dad 'Shawn', he wore red speedos and white footys on site everyday, I used to state at him whenever I was there 🫣

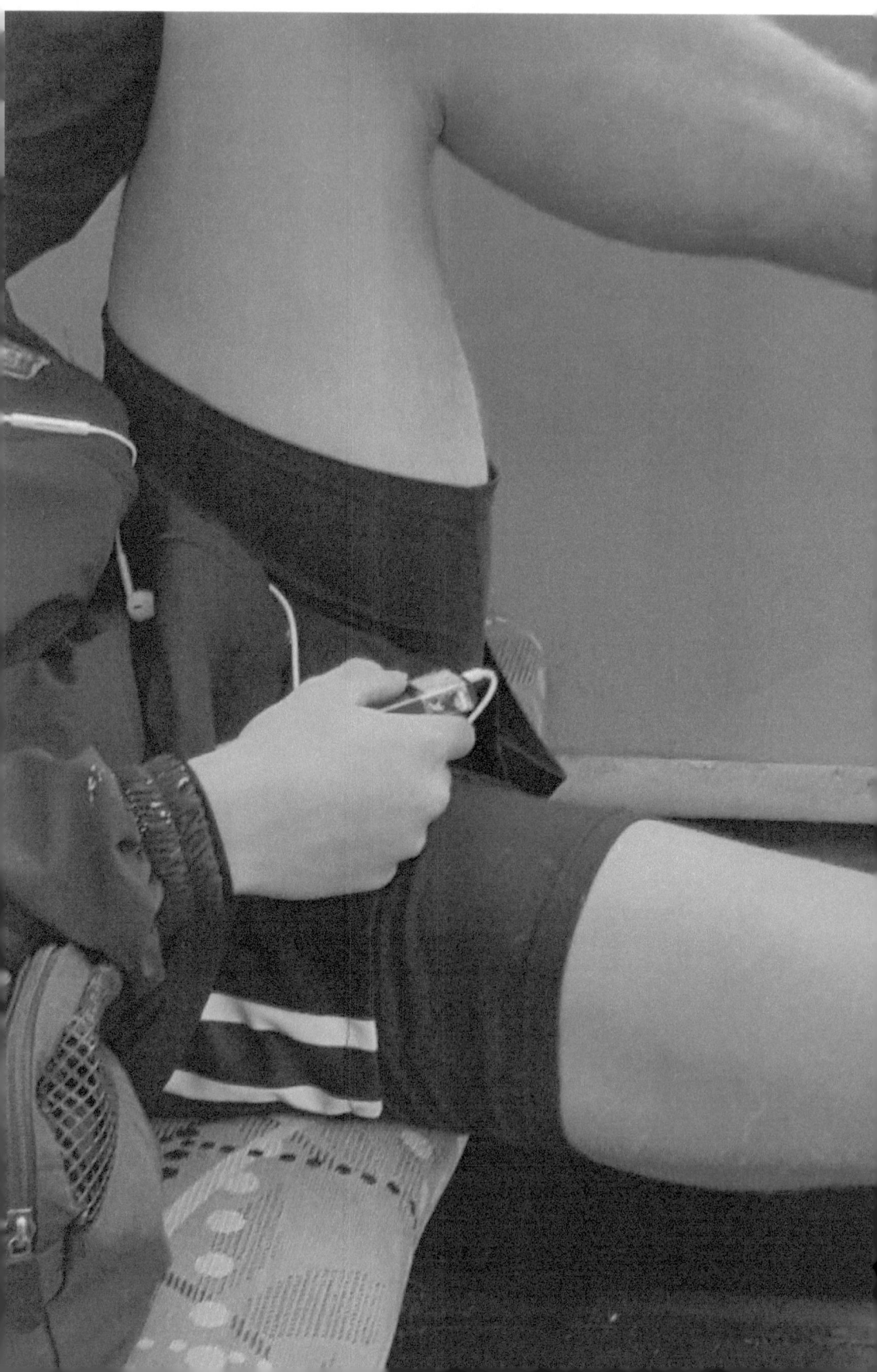

I LIVE IN FOOTY SHORTS AND AM NORMALLY GOING COMMANDO, I LOVE SPREADING MY LEGS ON THE TRAIN WHEN A HOT TRADIE IS ACROSS FROM ME, GIVE HIM A VIEW. SOMETIMES THEY SPREAD EM TOO.

I SAW MY BOSS AT THE
URINAL, COCK OUT THE
SIDE OF HIS FOOTYS, HARD
AS A ROCK

THE BLOKE NEXT DOOR IS A TRADIE AND WEARS PARTS SHORTS EVERYDAY TO WORK, I ONLYNINVITE HIM OVER FOR A BEER TO PERV, HE IS AS DUMB AS ROCKS.

My brother caught me jacking off and I knew he was watching

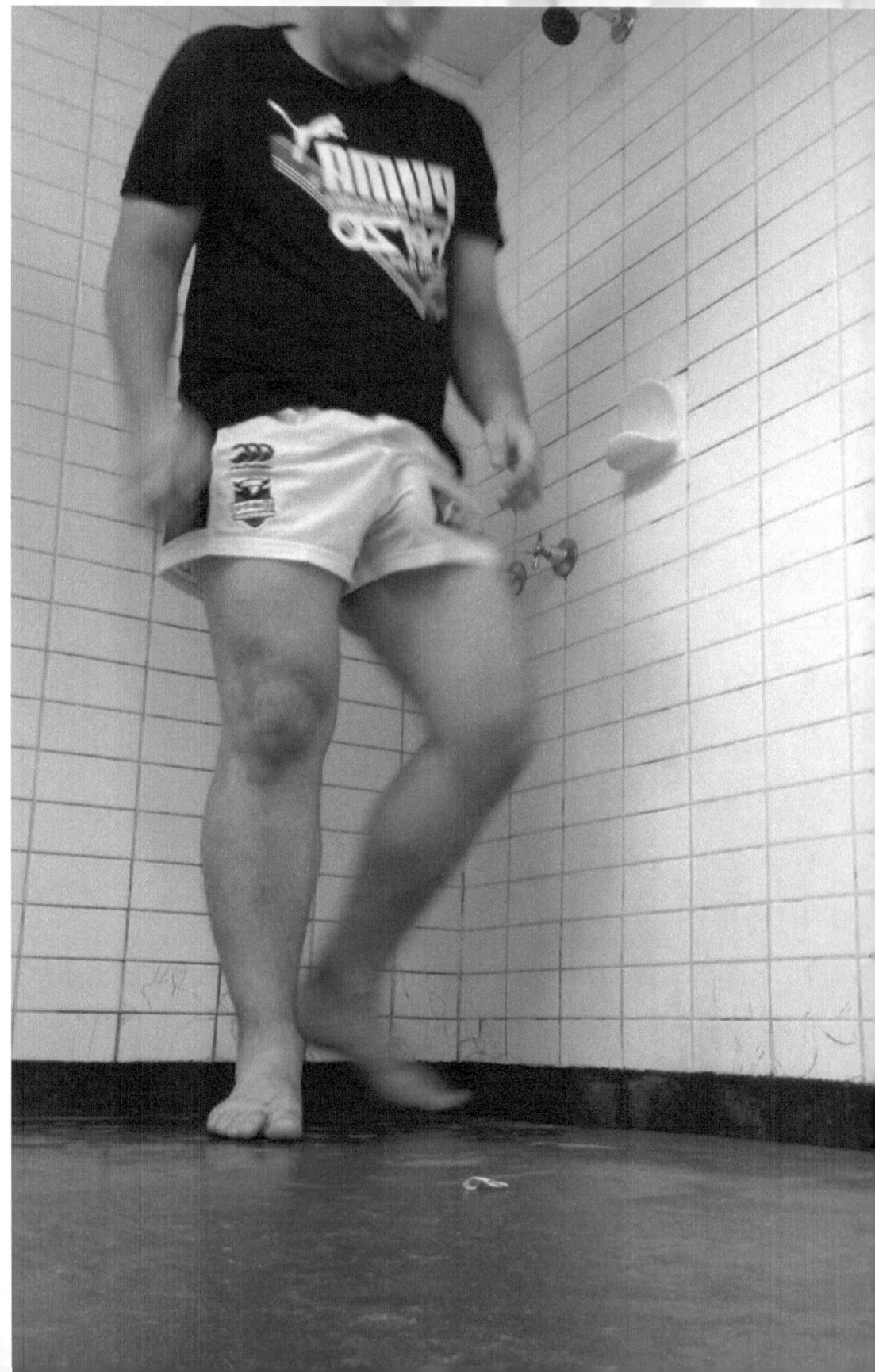

I SIGNED UP FOR THIS
HOT PERSONAL TRAINER AT
THE GYM CAUSE HE WEARS
WHITE FOOTYS AND SWEATS
LIKE A PIG, NEED I SAY
MORE

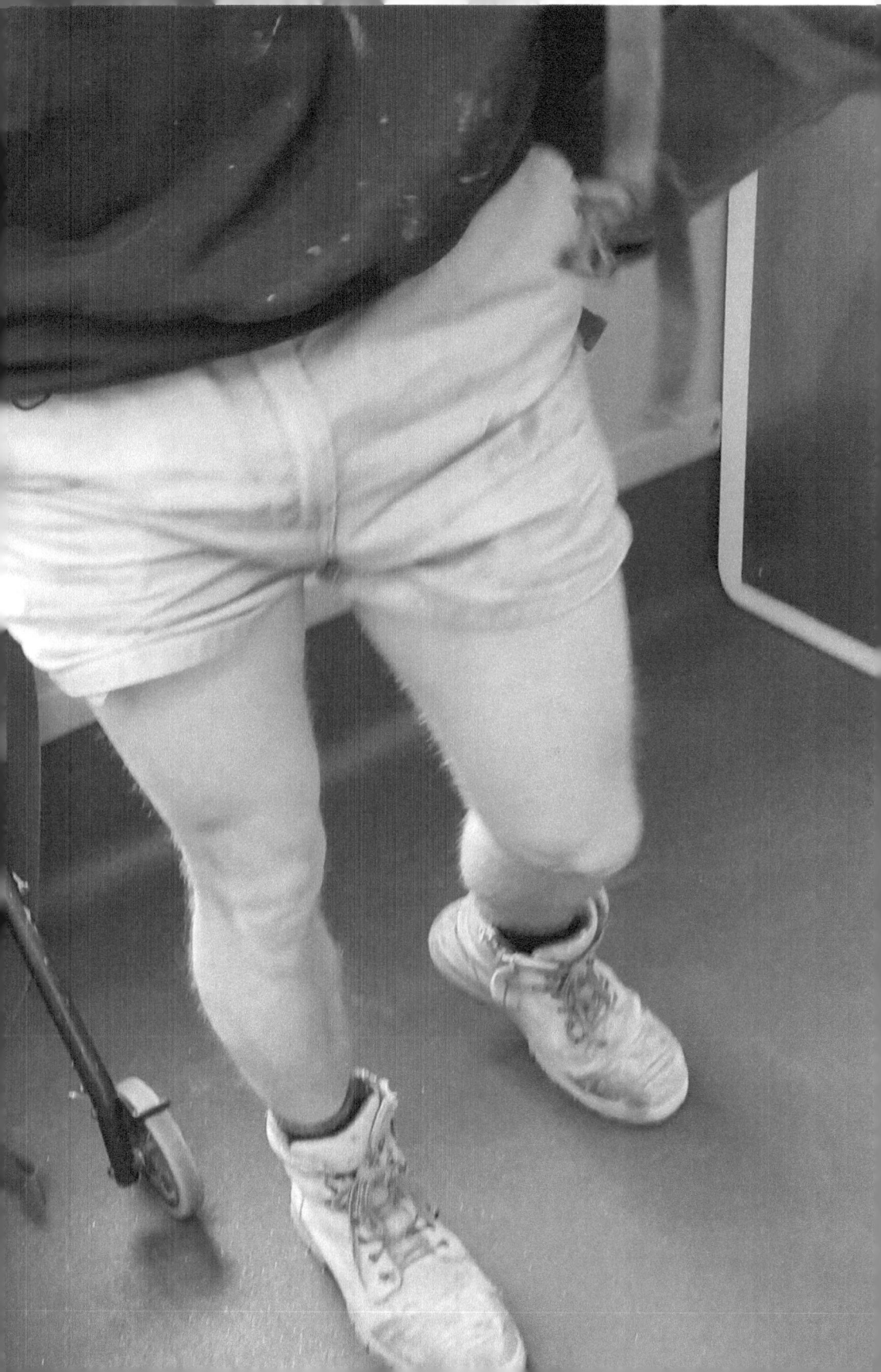